Religion and Place in Leed

Religion and Place in Leeds

John Minnis with Trevor Mitchell

Published by English Heritage, Kemble Drive, Swindon SN2 2GZ

www.english-heritage.org.uk

English Heritage is the Government's statutory adviser on all aspects of the historic environment.

© English Heritage 2007

Printing 10 9 8 7 6 5 4 3 2 1

Images (except as otherwise shown) © English Heritage or © Crown copyright. NMR.

First published 2007

ISBN 978-1-905624-48-5

Product code 51337

British Library Cataloguing in Publication data

A CIP catalogue record for this book is available from the British Library.

The National Monuments Record is the public archive of English Heritage. For more information, contact NMR Enquiry and Research Services, National Monuments Record Centre, Kemble Drive, Swindon SN2 2GZ; telephone (01793) 414600.

Brought to publication by Joan Hodsdon, Publishing, English Heritage.

Edited by Karl Sharrock
Page layout by Simon Borrough

Printed in the UK by Cambridge University Press.

This publication was supported by a grant from the Leeds Philosophical and Literary Society.

Front cover *The east end of Headingley St Columba United Reformed Church (1966, W & A Tocher), one of the most striking nonconformist churches of the period, is reminiscent of the prow of a great battleship. [DP027104]*

Inside front cover *The Greek Orthodox Church of the Three Hierarchs has successfully adapted the former Harehills Primitive Methodist Chapel (1902, W Hugill Dinsley) for a new use, adding the iconostasis seen here as the centrepiece of its worship. [DP029156]*

Frontispiece *Bilal Mosque, Harehills Lane (1999), designed by Atba Al-Samarraie, who believes strongly in the need to retain traditional Islamic symbols such as the green dome and the minaret in mosque architecture. [DP027129]*

vi *Chiselled coloured glass by Pierre Fourmaintreaux at St Nicholas, Gipton. [DP029187]*

Contents

Acknowledgements

Firstly, to my colleagues at English Heritage: Trevor Mitchell for contributing the chapter on conservation; Kathryn Morrison, John Cattell, Sarah Brown, Paul Barnwell and Richard Halsey for reading the manuscript and making many helpful suggestions; our photographic team, Steve Cole, Bob Skingle and Keith Buck; and for the aerial photography, Dave MacLeod.

In Leeds, I would like to thank Richard Taylor, Conservation Team Leader at Leeds City Council, and his team, and Nadir Khan of the Planning Department. I also thank Zoe Kemp formerly at the Churches Regional Commission for Yorkshire and the Humber, Mo Elliott, the Black Majority Churches Co-ordinator, Peter Mojsa of the Diocese of Ripon and Leeds, Robert Finnigan of the Catholic Diocese of Leeds, and David Figures of the United Reformed Church. Special thanks are due to Colin Dews who has generously made available the results of many years of research into the Methodist chapels of Leeds. Susan Lang carried out valuable initial research. Sharman Kadish of Jewish Heritage UK gave much help with the synagogues. Charles Sewell, Roger Shaw and Geoffrey Bass helped with individual churches. Finally, thanks to all the ministers and members of the management committees of the places of worship that were visited during the course of research for this book.

Foreword

Leeds has enjoyed a renaissance over the past 15 years; its role as a centre for business, finance and law has gone from strength to strength. The tangible results are evident in the new building rising ever outwards from the city centre, in the new offices, and in the housing, restaurants and shops that are brought into being by that commercial success.

But Leeds is not just concerned with material prosperity. In the past, the strength of its nonconformist, Anglican, Catholic and Jewish communities has been fundamental to the city's success. Today, a vibrant mix of cultures and faiths further enriches this legacy. Religious and cultural diversity has been a key feature of the city stretching back almost 200 years and has resulted in the building of many fine churches, chapels and synagogues; these are now being joined by striking mosques, Sikh gurdwaras and a Hindu mandir. The changing nature of faith in Leeds is reflected in the falling numbers of active worshippers in the Christian and Jewish faiths and the growing numbers in faiths established in the city since 1945, and in the challenges that these demographic changes bring. The very success of the city brings about pressures to redevelop to accommodate the increasing demand for housing, shops and offices.

At one time Leeds saw many fine redundant places of worship demolished; today care is taken to ensure that viable new uses, either by other denominations or faiths or for secular purposes, are found for them. For these buildings represent something important to communities – they hold memories of significant events in many people's lives and help to make places special. Indeed, in the suburbs and inner city areas with which this book is concerned, such buildings are often the most prominent structures. This book, which is based on work carried out by English Heritage's Research Department, looks at what has happened to places of worship in Leeds over the 20th century and examines the buildings that have been constructed since 1900. By knowing more about these buildings we can understand their place in people's lives and ensure that they survive as markers or signposts to the communities of which they form so important a part.

Simon Thurley
Chief Executive
English Heritage

Councillor Ann Castle
Historic Environment Champion
Leeds City Council

1

Introduction

The religious history of Leeds is remarkable in many ways. It is by far the largest English city not to have an Anglican diocese or cathedral; the Diocese of Ripon did not have Leeds added to its title until 1999. Until 1844 it was, like a number of northern cities, a single large parish which failed to take account of the vast growth in population as it transformed from market town to industrial city. As a result, the Anglican Church seemed increasingly remote from the lives of many working people, which greatly aided the expansion of nonconformity – a dominant factor in the city's religious life by the 19th century.

Leeds is also notable for the great length of time over which it has attracted immigrants from a great variety of ethnic, religious and geographical backgrounds. It has seen great waves of immigration, beginning with the Irish Catholics in the 1820s, then Jews from the 1860s and in large numbers from the 1880s, and, after 1945, Catholics from Poland, Pentecostals from the Caribbean, Muslims from Pakistan, Bangladesh and the Middle East, and Hindus and Sikhs from India and East Africa, among others. In this book, we look at how the architectural expression of faith in Leeds has changed from the inception of the 20th century to the present and how places of worship relate to their setting in the city. How are changing religious practices accommodated within buildings that were built in another age with different expectations and aspirations?

The book's focus is on the suburbs rather than the centre. The places of worship in the city centre enjoy a reasonably secure future, but those in both the inner and outer suburbs are seeing much more change in their neighbourhoods in terms of population decline, the ethnic and religious makeup of the areas and patterns of worship. Some may be no longer viable as places of worship and need new uses, which could change their appearance and affect their character. We therefore need to understand more about them and their history so that we can appreciate their quality and their contribution to the townscape of Leeds.

The Leeds edition of the Pevsner Architectural Guide series (2005) describes in detail many of the most outstanding 19th-century suburban churches – among them St Bartholomew in Armley, St Saviour in the Bank, St Aidan in Harehills and St Michael in Headingley, all buildings of

The early 20th century saw many additions to the furnishings and decoration of 19th-century churches. St Martin, Potternewton (1879–81, Adams & Kelly) had magnificent murals by Hemming & Co added in 1903. These depict both black and oriental angels, as if in unintentional recognition of the future cultural diversity of the Chapeltown area. The equally rich carved and gilded wooden reredos with its naturalistic figures also dates from the same period. English Heritage is funding investigative and repair works to this spectacular, yet little-known, church. [DP004212]

Beeston Hill, which grew rapidly between 1890 and 1910, epitomises how changes within a neighbourhood are reflected in its provision of places of worship. At the bottom in Hardy Street is the Kashmir Muslim Community Centre and Mosque, converted from a former co-op store; in the centre the Anglican church of the Holy Spirit (1903, Prothero & Phillott); and at the top facing Tempest Road, the former Trinity Methodist Church (1907, W S Braithwaite), whose congregation now meets in the multi-faith Building Blocks Centre, run in association with the Anglicans and two Muslim charities, located between it and Holy Spirit. [NMR 20668/022 24-AUG-2007 © English Heritage.NMR]

considerable national significance. Our concern here is to examine the lesser known but often fascinating churches, chapels and synagogues of the 20th century, to see what has happened to buildings of the established faiths over the past century, to look at the buildings associated with the faiths that have grown substantially in recent years and to consider how to conserve the legacy of Leeds' historic places of worship, especially those of the city's neglected nonconformist past.

If there is a bias in this book, it is towards the typical rather than the exceptional. Architectural history tends to be about the trend setters, the architects whose buildings marked new directions in architecture or those buildings that display exceptional craftsmanship. Because of this, thousands of buildings that have defined people's lives, that acted as the backdrop for key human events and that still have meaning for millions today are neglected. The mission church, the gospel hall and the mosque converted from a terraced house will receive attention, together with their architecturally more imposing counterparts.

Beth Hamedrash Hagadol. The premises in Bridge Street were opened in 1908 and described at the time as one of the largest synagogues outside London. Closure took place following the move northwards of the Jewish community away from the Leylands. (Courtesy of Leeds Library and Information Service, 2002319 4814875)

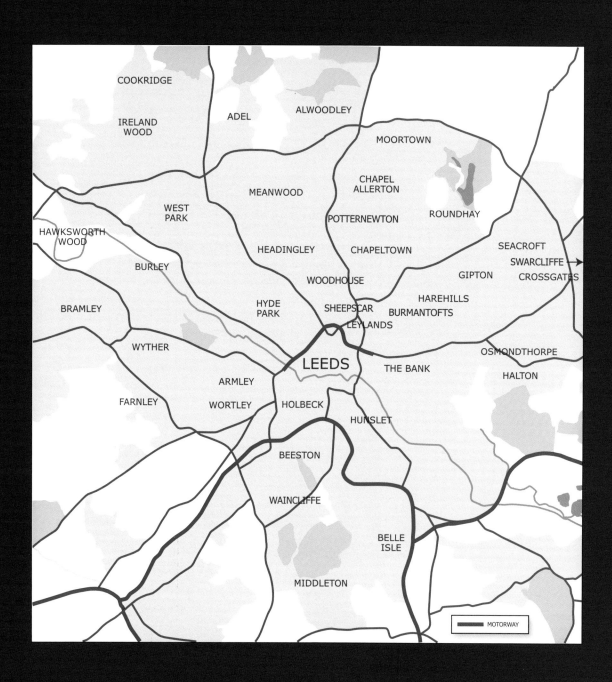

2

The geographical setting

The expansion of Leeds in the 19th and early 20th centuries did not follow the usual pattern in English cities of well-to-do suburbs on the west side and working class housing on the east. Instead, development was much more variegated, with extensive artisan housing to the west and most of the middle and upper class development to the north. What is unusual is how the rich and poor lived cheek by jowl, which to some extent they still do. Headingley, the premier suburb for much of the period, is bounded by the much poorer Hyde Park and Woodhouse. Roundhay, the high-status Edwardian suburb to the north-east, is close to the back-to-backs of Harehills. West Park, Roundhay's equivalent in the north-west, is less than a mile from the social housing of Hawksworth Wood.

The earliest and poorest suburbs were those immediately to the east, north and south of the centre. The Leylands, the Bank, Burmantofts, Holbeck and Hunslet had developed principally by the mid-19th century as a maze of irregular streets and courts, filled with blind-back and back-to-back cottages of the poorest sort, now completely cleared. Development continued further out from these areas but in a new and quite different form, with the irregular street patterns replaced by the opposite extreme of toast-racks of working class streets running end-on to the principal through roads. The red-brick terraces of back-to-back houses lining these streets formed the characteristic landscape of Leeds, much of it extant today as building of the type continued well into the 1900s. Among such areas were Beeston to the south, Harehills to the east, and Hyde Park, Burley and Armley to the west.

The prosperous suburbs expanded northwards as part of a process that began in the early 19th century at Potternewton, continued with Chapel Allerton and ended with development at Moortown and Alwoodley in the 1930s and 1950s. Between the wars expansion occurred on all sides of the city, taking in villages such as Halton and Crossgates to the east and Farnley to the west, and during the same period large housing estates such as Gipton and Middleton were built on the outskirts of the city to rehouse the city centre population.

Map of Leeds, showing the suburbs and motorways. (Drawn by George Wilson)

3

A Methodist city?

In the 19th century the parish church of St Peter, rebuilt by R D Chantrell between 1837 and 1841, was the focus of Anglicanism in Leeds, and its vicar was an extraordinarily powerful figure in the city, whose influence was as great as, if not greater than, that of his titular superior, the Bishop of Ripon. Into this post came Walter Hook in 1837, who served for some 20 years and whose mission was to arrest the movement of Leeds folk away from Anglicanism to nonconformity and, in particular, Methodism. Hook was besieged on all sides: from the Methodists, from the Evangelicals and, despite his own High Church inclinations, not shared by many in the diocese, from the Anglo-Catholics associated with St Saviour's, the church paid for by Edward Pusey, perhaps their most powerful advocate.

A wealth of churches and chapels

But Leeds was, by the early 19th century, a Methodist city; Hook himself wrote in 1837 that 'the de facto established religion is Methodism' (Hastings 1994). Although Hook revitalised Leeds Anglicanism, subdividing the enormous single parish in 1844 into smaller parishes and establishing over 20 new churches, the Methodists remained dominant in both numbers and political influence in the city. The 1851 religious census indicated that those attending church on the census Sunday were divided into three almost equal parts: the Anglicans, the Methodists and the other denominations. By 1905 there were 129 Methodist chapels in Leeds, although any claim to the term 'established' is negated by the inevitable tendency to schism, with the principal branches of Methodism – the Wesleyan Methodists, the Primitive Methodists, the United Methodist Free Churches and the Methodist New Connexion – all well represented. The situation led to the over-provision of chapels, and the reduction in their number began with the unions of 1907 and 1932.

By the end of the 19th century, Leeds had a wealth of churches and chapels, as befitted its new-found city status, granted in 1893. Many of the greatest names among church architects had carried out work there: William Butterfield, Sir George Gilbert Scott, G E Street, J L Pearson, J T Micklethwaite and G F Bodley were all represented by at least one church. The local architects too included many men of considerable

Churches in the newly-developed and prosperous suburb of Lidgett Park, Roundhay were given prominent positions at road junctions. They helped mark the evident respectability of the new community. Lidgett Park Methodist Church (1926, Arthur Brocklehurst & Co) on the left faces St Edmund's Anglican church (1908, W. Carby Hall) at the point where several roads meet. [NMR 20666/008 24-AUG-2007 © English Heritage.NMR]

talent: George Corson, Cuthbert Brodrick, R D Chantrell, Thomas Ambler, Chorley & Connon, Smith & Tweedale, Perkin & Backhouse. Beyond this first division, there was a string of architects who specialised in building chapels, often if not exclusively for one denomination: Adams & Kelly for the Roman Catholics, James Simpson for nonconformists, Thomas Howdill for the Primitive Methodists, G F Danby for the Wesleyan Methodists, and William Hill for Methodists of any persuasion.

Alongside these are the mission rooms intended to bring religion to the labouring classes, of which the Church of England alone had 29 in 1905, with a further 26 run by the nonconformist denominations or by independent groups, such as the Unsectarian Mission Room in Place's Road, the Bank, or the Highway Bible Mission in Oakwood Avenue, Roundhay. The heyday of the mission room was the 1890s, with the Leeds Church Extension Society, founded in 1864, enthusiastically supporting the demand. Most of them were located in the inner districts

Middleton Methodist Church (1896, Howdill & Howdill) has an increasingly rare intact late 19th-century chapel interior, retaining its pews, gallery and rostrum. [DP028581]

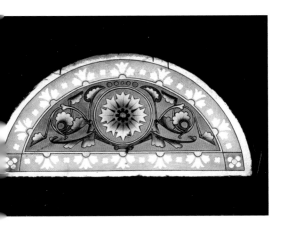

The glass in the upper parts of the side windows at Beeston Methodist Church bore charming foliage designs. [DP029113]

and have vanished – unsung and often unrecorded. They occupied a variety of buildings, some housed in corrugated iron halls, others in domestic houses, while a few had purpose-built brick structures. While few if any were of any architectural distinction, they represented a strand in working class religion that was once a vital force. A rare survivor is the former Holiness Church Mission Room in Dewsbury Road, Hunslet, now in commercial use.

The early immigrants

Immigration into the city was to be one of the defining characteristics of Leeds throughout the 19th and 20th centuries and remains so in the 21st. The first wave of immigrants had arrived from Ireland in the 1820s and settled immediately to the east of the city centre and in the area known as the Bank, later spreading out to Hunslet and Beeston. Leeds was the first town in England to have a Catholic mayor, in 1838–9. Irish immigration accelerated after the potato famine of 1846–7; and in 1861 nearly 15,000 people (almost all Catholics), or over 12 per cent of the population of Leeds, were of Irish origin. A Catholic diocese was established in 1862, but initially the number of churches constructed was relatively small, with only seven by the turn of the century.

Small numbers of Jewish people, mostly middle class merchants from Germany, settled in Leeds from the 1840s, and the Great Synagogue in Belgrave Street, close to the centre, was opened in 1861. A second wave of immigration started in the 1880s with the arrival of Jews from eastern Europe fleeing persecution. They settled just to the north of the centre in the Leylands and Sheepscar. They found the services at Belgrave Street too 'English' and formed new synagogues, known as 'Grinners' ('newcomers'), in the poor streets of the Leylands. By 1900, the Jewish community numbered around 15,000, the second largest outside London. As the community matured, its members gradually moved out in the early 20th century to Chapeltown and from the 1930s further north to Moortown. This movement explains the absence of any pre-1914 synagogues in Leeds. They closed as the community moved north and were then demolished as part of the slum clearance programmes in the 1950s and 1960s.

4

New century, new challenges

Twentieth-century church building in Leeds has to be seen within the context of changes in liturgy and, in particular, in the role of the Eucharist in Christian worship. To describe these developments in detail would fill this book; but essentially, at the turn of the century, communion or mass was celebrated by the priest facing the high altar, which was placed against the east wall of a lengthy chancel, and thus he would have his back to the congregation. The congregation's view of the Sacrament would generally be obscured by a choir placed between them and the altar and often by a rood screen as well. Since the 1930s, the emphasis has been on involving the congregation in the Eucharist as participants rather than as spectators, by reducing the space between priest and congregation, generally by bringing the altar forward so that it is within the nave of the church rather than at the remote east end, and with the priest facing the congregation. The emphasis on the Eucharist is what distinguishes Anglican and Catholic churches from most of the nonconformist denominations, where the focus is on preaching – hence the prominence they give to pulpits, which are often in a central position above a rostrum with the choir below, although some possess shallow chancels in the Anglican manner.

The new century initially brought little change in church building, but construction began to tail off, especially for the Anglicans, by about 1910. The shift from the centre of the city to the suburbs had already begun, and the Leeds Churches Act of 1901 recommended the demolition of three city churches and the rearrangement of parish boundaries. The number of churches and chapels in the city reached its highest around this time, with a total of over 270 in 1905. Although the number in the centre declined, this was at first matched by growth in construction in the expanding suburbs, where it often took the form of either a temporary building of timber or corrugated iron or reuse of an existing building, followed sometimes many years later by the construction of a permanent church when funds were available.

The pattern established in the late 19th century – of architects with a national reputation taking on prestigious Anglican churches, while churches of other denominations were principally the work of local specialists – continued.

The font of St Edmund, Roundhay (1908, W Carby Hall) by the church suppliers Jones & Willis of Birmingham, typical of the rich furnishings of this large church at the heart of a well-to-do Edwardian suburb. [DP020986]

Poor location led to the closure of two of Leeds' finest Edwardian churches. St Edward, Holbeck by G F Bodley, of 1903–4, was located on the edge of a working class district and provided by High Church philanthropy. Bodley had recently designed St Matthew, Chapel Allerton, and St Edward was to be his last church, built in red brick and distinguished by a vast and magnificent reredos (now at Christchurch, Moss Side, Manchester). It was built in anticipation of the suburb growing, but in practice the land around it was used for industry, and the church, like many Anglican churches of the period, never succeeded in attracting a sufficiently large congregation. St Edward's destruction in 1982 was a considerable loss.

Temple Moore's St Margaret of Antioch, Cardigan Road, Hyde Park (1908–9) was built on a grand scale in red brick in that architect's typically muscular style and strong massing. It too served a working class area and was located in a poor position away from any natural centre and opposite a railway goods yard. Its west end was never completed and it was not until 1964 that a permanent west front was added by George Pace. The design, the most visible part of the church, continues to divide public opinion today.

In strong contrast, in the heart of Beeston Hill is the Arts and Crafts influenced Holy Spirit by Prothero and Phillott of Cheltenham (1903), which sits a little uneasily in its harshly urban setting of terraced houses. It is in the late Perpendicular style much favoured by nonconformists at the time and forms a group with the neighbouring former Trinity Methodist church of 1907 by the Leeds architect W S Braithwaite, which eschews Perpendicular for the Decorated style. An imposing church with a spire, Trinity was the last church to be built for the Methodist New Connexion prior to their union with the United Methodist Free Churches and Bible Christians in 1907 and shows how far they had come from the Classical chapels of the mid-19th century.

A further comparison between denominations is possible at Roundhay, where Methodist and Anglican churches are on opposite corners of the junction of a number of broad roads and a Congregational church was built nearby. Although all three churches vie with one another for attention, the area is heavily wooded and they almost disappear

St Andrew's United Reformed Church, built as Roundhay Congregational Church in 1907 (W H Beevers) in a fashionable neo-Perpendicular style that expresses the self-confidence of the Congregationalists who built it. [DP027720]

amongst the verdure in summer. Roundhay was developed at the beginning of the 20th century as one of Leeds' finest suburbs and its churches reflect the wealth of its residents. The three churches are all large and ambitiously designed and remain thriving to the present day, cherished by their congregations and working in close partnership with one another. All three began with the construction of a hall and schools, with the churches following as funds were raised. Roundhay Congregational Church (now St Andrew's United Reformed Church) was opened in 1907, its architect W H Beevers designing many of the surrounding houses and himself living in one just up the road from the church. St Andrew's is in a free Perpendicular style and gains much from a fine tower (*previous page*). Beevers also designed the hall and schools of Lidgett Park Wesleyan Methodist Church in a similar Perpendicular style, but the church itself was not built until 1926 and by a different practice, the Lancashire-based church specialists Arthur Brocklehurst & Co. The Anglican church was another case where the architect was involved in local estate development. W Carby Hall was a designer of houses and shopping parades, but in 1908 he produced what was to be his only church, St Edmund, a large structure that again took many years to complete. Its chancel was not built until 1933–5 and the intended tower, which would have been a landmark for the district, never rose above its base. The church was planned on a grand scale with rich furnishings (*see* p 10) and stained glass. It is a valiant effort and undeniably impressive, but Carby Hall's shortcomings are seen in the curious proportions of the clerestory.

At the opposite end of the scale, one of the last mission churches to be built – and today a rare survivor – was St Hugh, built by the eminent local practice of Chorley & Connon in 1908–9 within a tight cluster of back-to-backs in Armley known as 'The Aviaries'. Derelict for some years, it is being refurbished as housing.

Catholic expansion was slow during this period, at least in terms of construction of new churches, with the building of St Anne's Cathedral taking up most of the energies of the diocese. Only one other church was built during the period, St Anthony of Padua, to serve the Catholics of

Cemetery Road Baptist Church, Beeston (now City Evangelical Church) by Walter A Hobson (1901), a building whose size fits it well for its present large congregation. [DP027092]

the rapidly expanding south part of Beeston that was growing up around Cross Flatts Park with superior (that is, not back-to-back) houses. St Anthony (1904), on a prominent corner site, was an entirely conventional design in red brick with an apsidal east end by the Leeds practice of Kelly & Birchall, responsible for most of the city's 19th-century Catholic churches and very similar in arrangement to Kelly's Holy Family, Armley of 1894–5.

The nonconformists were much more prolific, continuing to replace existing chapels and to build new ones to minister to the expanding outer suburbs. The Churches of Christ built a back-street mission chapel in Gledhow Road, Sheepscar in a simple Renaissance style in 1900. Designed by J W Thackray, it survives with its plain interior unaltered. Much grander was Cemetery Road Baptist Church at Beeston Hill, standing on the crest of the hill and overlooking the city centre. This had

The original school church at Harehills Lane Baptist Church (1906–7, Cubitt & Manchip) has extraordinary 'borrowed lights' – the smaller, lower windows – to throw light into the aisles. [DP029154]

originally been designed in Gothic style by Walter A Hobson, and plans were passed by the City Council in 1897. However, for some reason (probably cost, as Gothic was always reckoned to cost substantially more than Classical), it was decided instead to build in the Classical style. Hobson prepared a fresh set of plans with the layout of the building unchanged, and the chapel was built in this form in 1901. The building is of considerable size, with a large ground floor hall and many classrooms, which, with its balcony, is well suited to the 400-strong congregation attending what is now the City Evangelical Church.

The move of the Baptists from their city centre location at South Parade was marked by the creation of new buildings at Headingley and at Harehills, both of some distinction. At Headingley, the congregation persuaded the City Council to rename the road outside the new church South Parade in recognition of their long occupation of their former premises. In 1908 a large building in a stylish and eclectic Gothic and housing a hall and schools was designed by the gifted Percy Robinson (who was acclaimed for his picturesque sketches of old Leeds) and W A Jones. An offshoot of South Parade at Harehills Lane was provided with similar accommodation by the London practice of Cubitt & Manchip in 1906–7, 'Cubitt' being the noted nonconformist architect James Cubitt. The hall at Harehills Lane was particularly striking, with 'borrowed' light from the nave through small paned casements to light the aisles (*opposite*). As with South Parade, it was not until after the First World War that the church was built, by Herbert Manchip, Cubitt's successor in the partnership. In both cases, the halls were built facing side roads, leaving the primary position on the main road for the church.

Harehills grew very rapidly at the turn of the century and two churches were built on Harehills Road in close proximity. The Catholics put up a temporary building dedicated to St Augustine, while in 1900–1 the Congregationalists built a new church designed by Tom Dyer on the prominent main road site in front of their hall of 1891. This survives in community use although it has lost the spire that made it a landmark. Less striking were the schools and hall on Dewsbury Road, Beeston that now form Dewsbury Road United Reformed Church, which Danby & Simpson designed in 1908. Danby usually designed for the Wesleyan Methodists, but like many of the Leeds architects he did not work exclusively for one denomination. Space was left for a permanent church on the corner but, as so often happened, it was never built and the hall became the church.

More provision for expanding suburbs could be seen elsewhere in Harehills, where two large chapels were sited on tree-lined Harehills Avenue, the premier road in Harehills that ran alongside Potternewton Park, newly purchased for the city. In a prime position facing the park was Trinity Presbyterian Church, another progressive Gothic essay by W H Beevers of 1906 and coming close to Anglican planning with a clearly differentiated chancel. Nearby stands the equally imposing Primitive Methodist chapel (now the Greek Orthodox Church of the Three Hierarchs (*see* inside front cover) of 1902, broadly Perpendicular Gothic in style, with a large hall to the rear. The architect was W Hugill Dinsley of Chorley, Lancashire, whose practice 30 years later designed Stainbeck Congregational.

While the majority of chapels conformed to broadly Gothic designs by the early 20th century, there were plenty of exceptions. Armley, another working class district that grew considerably in the 1890s, saw a spate of chapel building and is the one part of Leeds where the traditional tight-knit relationship between chapel and terraced housing may still be observed. The United Methodist Free Church in Hall Road (*opposite*) was opened in 1900 and was the work of Walter Hanstock & Son, who had made a name for themselves as designers of municipal buildings, especially markets and swimming baths. Hanstock reused some elements of his long-since demolished Leeds Meat Market in the design, notably in the two towers. The rounded gable that links them is in some ways preposterous, but the building, in the Free Renaissance style and with its Florentine side windows, has tremendous character that helps to 'lift' the neighbourhood. Charles Howdill, who had joined his father Thomas in partnership, also employed a flamboyant northern Renaissance style for the Primitive Methodist chapel he designed at Stanningley Road, Armley, opened in 1905. Marking the edge of Armley township centre, it exploits its corner site with twin ventilation towers establishing a vertical emphasis, and its handsome Venetian window grabs the eye. Like Hall Road, the building is today a carpet warehouse, disfigured by intrusive signs. Thomas Howdill, who had been the leading architect for the Primitive Methodists in Leeds from the 1870s, had hitherto generally favoured Gothic, but evidently his son followed more progressive tastes, and there was nothing so progressive as the Free Renaissance at the turn of the 20th century.

*The former United Methodist Free Church in Hall
Road, Armley (1900, Walter Hanstock & Son) is a
building of great character that provides a focal point
for the streets around it. [DP028674]*

5

The move to the suburbs

Between the wars one of the most striking changes in Leeds' religious demography was the move of its Jewish population from the centre to Chapeltown, marked triumphantly by the building of the New Synagogue by J Stanley Wright in 1929–32 (*see* p 79). Built for the United Hebrew Congregation (formed from a merger of the New Briggate Synagogue, St John's Place and the Great Synagogue, Belgrave Street, both located a little to the north of the city centre), it was located close to other important Jewish facilities such as the Jewish Institute and Jubilee Hall (1934) and the kosher shops on Chapeltown Road. A large central dome is balanced by smaller domes above the stair towers either side of the entrance. This arrangement is emphasised by a Portland stone portico with tulip-leaf capitals on its paired columns, all in a neo-Egyptian style. Internally, the great open space of the shul (prayer hall) has survived conversion to the Northern School of Contemporary Dance in 1995–8 and retains the Star of David, from which a large pendant light is suspended. Other synagogues were built in Chapeltown; but in the same way as the move from the Leylands resulted in the destruction of the early synagogues, so too the postwar move to Moortown led to the loss of those in Chapeltown, and the only other survivor is the former Chadssidishe shul, off Spencer Place, a simple brick structure of 1934, externally having much in common with a gospel hall.

The First World War marked the start of a lengthy pause in church building in Leeds. The city was well provided, if not overly so, with churches, and there was no need to make additional provision until the end of the 1920s. Subsequently, inner areas were cleared – notably the Leylands and parts of the Bank to the north and east of the centre and Holbeck and Hunslet to the south – and slum dwellings were replaced by large new council estates on the outskirts of the city. The principal estates were at Belle Isle, Middleton, Wyther, Hawksworth Wood, Moor Allerton, Gipton and Osmondthorpe.

The Burroughs Commission

At the same time, the first major closures of inner city churches began as their parishes became depopulated. The changing situation led Bishop Burroughs to appoint a commission to investigate the question. As a

The deceptively simple lines of St Augustine, Harehills (1937, Gribbon, Foggitt & Brown) owe much to contemporary North European influence. [DP029162]

result, the Church Forward Movement was established in 1930 with an appeal for £100,000 to create churches in the new suburbs. In some cases, there were tangible links between the new churches and those that they replaced, with one church, for example, being literally removed from its central site and rebuilt on a new estate, albeit for a different denomination.

The first Anglican church to go up between the wars was a throwback. St Wilfrid, Harehills, which stands in an isolated position marking almost exactly the edge of pre-First World War building in the area, had been designed in 1913 by Sydney Kitson, but because of the war, work did not begin until 1927. The design had been modified by James Parish, although it remained broadly in the Arts and Crafts tradition. Even more firmly in that tradition was the last church by one of the masters of the Arts and Crafts style, W D Caröe, built to serve the new Hawksworth Wood estate to which it is curiously unrelated, being somewhat tucked away on the periphery. St Mary of 1932–3 is a small church of great delicacy displaying fine craftsmanship. Most unusually for the West Riding of Yorkshire, it is built of flint incorporating flushwork in the East Anglian manner. It was paid for by H M Butler, a director of the Kirkstall Forge, the principal employer in the area. Two alternative explanations for the use of flint are that Butler believed the material was far better in resisting the depredations of the sooty atmosphere than millstone grit and that his wife came from Norfolk and it evoked happy memories. The material proved very difficult for the local builders to work, and it became necessary to bring in flint knappers from Norfolk to complete the work. Caröe adopted the Arts and Crafts belief that an architect should design everything within a building and designed a magnificent rood screen and choir stalls, each terminating in carved angels. He adopted the 'unity by inclusion' approach associated with Ninian Comper, mixing Gothic with Renaissance scrolls and turned shafts in the woodwork and unifying the interior by continuing the scroll motif in the pulpit and font. Every detail is carefully considered, and Butler, the client, in a personal letter called it 'a gem of a church', a verdict with which it is hard to disagree.

The font of St Mary, Hawksworth Wood displays how Caröe skilfully combined Classical and Gothic motifs in a harmonious composition. [DP027037]

Every detail of the interior of St Mary, Hawksworth Wood (1932–3, W D Caröe) was designed by the architect and is of superb quality. [DP027036]

The churches built under Bishop Burroughs' campaign made much more of an impact on the landscape. The size of the estates was felt to warrant large buildings on prominent sites that were made available by the City Council for what in many instances were the only interruptions to the somewhat monotonous rows of small two-storey houses. F L Charlton was responsible for two churches serving the new estates: St Philip, Osmondthorpe of 1932–3 (*below*) and St Cross (*opposite*), completed in 1935, serving the vast Middleton estate. St Philip is outwardly conventional in red brick, with round-headed windows in the Early Christian style much favoured by the Catholics and, to a lesser extent, the other denominations in the 1920s and 1930s. But this skin is supported on striking parabolic-arched concrete trusses that spring from the foundations to span the nave and take the whole weight of the roof. The unplastered trusses give the interior a powerful simplicity which focuses attention on the excellent woodwork by Robert Thompson of Kilburn. St Cross is more markedly Early Christian to the extent that it resembles contemporary Catholic churches, with an almost detached

The bold concrete arches of St Philip, Osmondthorpe (1932–3, F L Charlton) set up a rhythm that becomes the most striking feature of the building, radically different from previous conceptions of a church interior. [DP020990]

F L Charlton also designed St Cross, Middleton, and this view taken in 1935 shows how it was constructed using a series of concrete arches. To the right may be seen the temporary building that preceded it, typical of how many suburban churches started life. (Courtesy of St Cross)

north-east campanile (which acted as a powerful visual focus in predominantly flat surroundings) and rows of closely spaced windows in the clerestory. It too has roof trusses of concrete but these are combined with conventional side aisles and arcades.

A move towards a modernist agenda was made by the local practice of Gribbon, Foggitt & Brown in three particularly large churches, all of brick: the Venerable Bede, Wyther (1938) and SS John and Barnabas, Belle Isle (1938–9) for the Anglicans, and St Augustine, Harehills Road (1937) for the Catholics (*see* p 20 and p 26). St Augustine replaced an existing temporary church in an area developed in the first decades of the 20th century; the other two churches both served new estates.

The interior of St Augustine, Harehills showing the exposed concrete framing and the remodelling of the sanctuary carried out by Derek Walker in 1960. [DP029164]

St Augustine has a lengthy nave with the chancel all under a single roof, the nave walls being articulated by slim angled buttresses and very deep paired windows. Reinforced-concrete roof trusses carry a four-centred roof and give the interior a dramatic open character.

The Venerable Bede is externally the most determinedly modern of the three, showing the influence of the widely published architects Francis Xavier Velarde and N F Cachemaille-Day, and is the only one to have a tower instead of a bellcote. It stands high above the main road to Bradford and is built on a substantial undercroft covering the whole area of the church and housing a Sunday school and choir vestry. The architects exploited bold, massive rectangular forms with much uninterrupted brickwork and minimal decoration. In contrast, the interior has stark unmoulded Gothic arches in a continuous curve from the apex of the arch to the floor, separating the nave from the aisles and chancel.

The vicar of SS John and Barnabas was Charles Jenkinson, a priest-politician who, as chairman of the council's Housing Committee from 1933 to 1936, was the key figure in the city's programme of slum clearance. His

Vicarage

Church

Vestry

Hall

Family Centre entrance

Family Centre in crypt

St John and St Barnabas (1938–9, Gribbon, Foggitt & Brown) was built as a complex intended by Charles Jenkinson to cater for both the spiritual and intellectual needs of his parishioners in the new Belle Isle housing estate. The tradition has continued with the incorporation of the Family Centre in the crypt of the church. (Drawing by Allan Adams)

achievements included the creation of Quarry Hill Flats, the planning of
many new housing estates and rent rebate schemes. Jenkinson was
appointed vicar of the combined parishes of SS John and Barnabas in
Holbeck in 1927 and, over the next few years, much of his congregation
was rehoused in Belle Isle. He and the Bishop of Ripon agreed a scheme
whereby the inner city parish would fall within that of Christ Church,
Meadow Lane and its benefice income used to support the new parish of
the same name in Belle Isle. The new church retains many fittings and
furnishings from its predecessors: the pulpit, choir stalls, organ and some
pews from St John and the font from St Barnabas, together with much
stained glass, reset in clear glass windows. The church is part of a range of
facilities that Jenkinson saw as vital to re-establishing a sense of community
among the rehoused city dwellers. These included a hall, school, library and
a crypt, converted in 2002 to a family centre. The church, vicarage and hall
form a massive T-shaped block, impressive in its massing if a little
forbidding in appearance. Externally, it is austere, the west end, dominated
by a large cross executed in the brickwork, having only two windows
(*previous page*). Deep windows give a great deal of light, a particular
concern of Jenkinson's; he saw the lack of light in the cramped courts of
Holbeck as one of the worst aspects of the lives of working people. The
brightness is increased by the interior being completely open: there are no
piers or other divisions within the body of the church.

Two other churches completed in 1938 to serve expanding residential
areas are major works of architects nationally renowned for their church
building. Both were funded by Sir John Priestman, a Sunderland ship
builder, who made a gift of £20,000 to the Ripon diocese in 1937, but
their style and plan form an instructive contrast. The Church of the
Epiphany, Gipton is by N F Cachemaille-Day, who was responsible for
some of the most avant-garde churches of the 1930s. The Epiphany ranks
among his most significant works alongside St Nicholas, Burnage,
Manchester and St Saviour, Eltham, south London. Cachemaille-Day
initially proposed a simple rectangular church but this was changed,
following a visit to the great Romanesque cathedral at Coutances, France,
to the present more dramatic composition, which derives maximum
benefit from its prominent site on a junction of several roads on the

*A real powerhouse of faith: the Church of the Epiphany
extends eastwards with projections inspired by the great
French cathedral at Coutances. (NMR English
Heritage Herbert Felton Collection, CC47 02115)*

*The dramatic interior of N F Cachemaille-Day's
Church of the Epiphany, Gipton, photographed soon
after construction in 1938. (NMR English Heritage
Herbert Felton collection, CC47 02117)*

Subsequent additions to St Wilfrid such as this relief panel, forming a part of the Mysteries of the Rosary set by Irene Payne (1947), have further enhanced the building. [DP035626]

St Wilfrid, Halton (1939, Randall Wells) vies with the Church of the Epiphany as the most impressive inter-wars church in Leeds. The Gothic inspiration is clear but is handled in a Modernist manner. English Heritage is funding investigative works and repairs to the church. [DP035620]

Gipton council estate. To the junction the church presents its fortress-like east end, a mass of sweeping and receding curves, its seeming impenetrability broken only by tall thin windows. This stepped-up east end displays the influence of Coutances: a deep, apsed Lady chapel, a higher semicircular ambulatory behind and a yet higher pitched nave roof behind a heavy parapet. The reinforced concrete frame is clad in red brick, while heavy parapets and continuous string courses are remarkably successful in balancing the strong vertical emphasis.

The interior, originally with walls and ceilings of unconcealed concrete, now painted white, has 18m-high concrete piers supporting flat ceilings. The move of altars from the east wall of the chancel to the nave favoured in the late 20th century is anticipated in the sanctuary, which is slightly elevated on a circular plinth and is within the body of the nave. Even more dramatic is the raising of the Lady chapel above the altar, making it visible from the nave, an arrangement developed from that at St Nicholas, Burnage, and, on the same level, the positioning of the choir galleries facing the nave. Jazzy stained glass by Christopher Webb provides the only decoration.

Priestman was instrumental in securing A Randall Wells as architect of St Wilfrid, Halton (1939). Wells had been an assistant to two of the leading architects working in the Arts and Crafts style, W R Lethaby and E S Prior, and was the site architect of Prior's masterpiece, St Andrew, Roker, Sunderland, also funded by Priestman. St Wilfrid (his last building) can be interpreted as the ultimate development of his highly individualistic strand of Arts and Crafts. It replaced a mission church of 1888 and Lord Halifax donated an elevated site high up above the Selby Road, where it seems to float above the 1930s semi-detached houses. In contrast to all the other Leeds churches of the 1930s, it was built in Yorkshire stone and was broadly cruciform in shape. Grouped windows alluding to stepped early English lancets and groined vaults provided no more than a veneer of Gothic form to what was essentially a modernist church (*opposite*). The pointed windows and the surprisingly rustic, short timber spire with its many cross gables, which surmounts the blocky crossing tower, give the building a spiky character that is a little at odds with the massing of the nave and tower.

The interior is much more restful, brilliantly lit through clear glass and painted a cool white with simple unmoulded arches that act as a foil for Wells's innovative woodwork, whose closely set turned balusters provide much of the decoration within the church. The lighting comes from high up, all the windows being above narrow passage aisles, and above all is the roof, the vaulting so steep that it resembles an upturned ship.

The common factor in all the large Anglican churches of the 1930s is their response to the Parish Communion movement, which emphasised communion as a community feast rather than as an individual act. Altars were no longer hidden away at the east end but placed in spacious and highly visible sanctuaries, which anticipated the liturgical changes of the 1960s and lent themselves to the new patterns of worship that were evolving at that time.

Roman Catholic and nonconformist churches between the wars

The Roman Catholics continued to expand in the period, doubling the number of their churches from 6 in 1914 to 12 by 1939. Besides St Augustine, mentioned earlier, the other large church, standing side by side with the New Synagogue on Chapeltown Road, was Holy Rosary (1936–7) by Martin & Burnett. Here, the Early Christian theme is stripped down to bold modernist forms. Perhaps the most interesting development was the purchase and physical removal of R D Chantrell's St Philip from its city centre location in Wellington Road to a new site on the Middleton estate in 1934. The intention had been to purchase fittings from St Philip's, whose redundancy as a result of the depopulation of inner Leeds had become apparent as early as 1900. However, the building was in such good condition that it was dismantled and re-erected almost exactly in its original form. While the relocation of fittings as had happened at St John and St Barnabas was not uncommon, the re-erection of an entire church was rare in the 1930s.

The nonconformist churches made much less of a contribution to the landscape of the new estates, being, in the main, self-effacing brick structures in a watered-down Gothic that retained the traditional chapel form of gable end facing the road. Gipton Methodist (1933), Osmondthorpe Methodist (1930s) and Middleton Park Baptist (1920s)

The delicate plasterwork of the South Parade Baptist Church, Headingley (1924–7, Jones & Stocks) is set in a highly stylised Gothic setting. [DP035626]

are typical examples. Even simpler were the gospel halls; the Gospel Hall, Hunslet (1932) evoked the austere faith of its founders with few concessions to architectural adornment, although the Elim Foursquare Gospel Alliance, Bridge Street (1930–1) by Arthur Brocklehurst & Co is more elaborate in a minimal neo-Georgian. More ambitious and all helped by being located on corner sites are Stainbeck Congregational (1930) by Dinsley & Moss, built as a hall and schools and Edwardian in character (Dinsley had done Harehills Avenue Primitive Methodist Chapel in 1902 (*see* inside front cover and pp 17–18)), Gribbon Foggitt & Brown's West Park Congregational (1937–8) and F L Charlton's Adel Methodist (1937), both nodding to modernism but without the funding to do anything very spectacular.

The impressive timber roof and Arts and Crafts-style windows by W F Clokey & Co are unexpected features of Lidgett Park Methodist Church (1926, Arthur Brocklehurst & Co). [DP028541]

But three churches stand out: South Parade Baptist Church, Headingley (1924–7) by Jones & Stocks, Lidgett Park Methodist (1926) by Arthur Brocklehurst & Co and Harehills Baptist Church, Harehills Lane (1928) by Herbert J Manchip. South Parade is in a free Gothic style with a steel truss roof disguised by an attractive plaster ceiling in a broad curve cut into by the clerestory windows (*see* p 33); while the exterior is Gothic, Renaissance motifs are to the fore inside. The broad lines of Lidgett Park had been set out before the First World War. It has an impressive Guiseley stone exterior with a 23m west tower, in vestigial Perpendicular, and is unusually richly furnished for a Methodist chapel. The dominant aspect of the interior is the hammerbeam roof with massive arched braces (*opposite*). Tracery is stylised and is complemented with fine Arts and Crafts stained glass by W F Clokey & Co of Belfast. Harehills Baptist is a full-blooded representation of Italian late Romanesque with heavy corbelling, a rose window and an elegant stone porch to the gabled west front. The cheerful red-brick and plaster interior has arcades of rounded arches supported on dumpy round piers with bell capitals and a domed baptistery at the east end.

6

Conservatism and practicality

Leeds did not suffer from bombing during the Second World War to the same extent as many other British cities and few churches were lost in this way. Church building ceased during the war years but after 1945 carried on along the same lines as those established before the war of catering for the new suburban estates, both public and private, and providing for the expansion of the Catholic population. There was little change in design either: the inter-wars trend of simple designs in brick, broadly Early Christian in style, was followed by the Anglican, Catholic and Congregational churches alike. Initially, building controls prevented much new construction, and most of the buildings put up prior to the removal of the controls in 1954 comprised simple structures that could be adapted as church halls when time and funds permitted. Examples are St Paul, Ireland Wood (1951) (*see* p 41 and pp 43–4) and a series of almost identical churches for the Catholics, St Paul (1952–3), Holy Name of Jesus (1953) and St Gregory, Swarcliffe (1954).

Catholic churches were almost entirely conservative in design, failing to follow the modernity of St Augustine, Harehills (*see* p 20 and p 26). St Theresa, Cross Gates (1953) and Our Lady of Good Counsel, Seacroft (1960) are well-proportioned essays in the Early Christian style, especially the latter with its tower more suggestive of Tuscan hill towns than the semi-detached homes of Seacroft. The Immaculate Heart of Mary, Harrogate Road, Moortown by R A Ronchetti (1956) is a more ambitious exercise. Leeds was by no means unique in its traditional approach; the northern Catholic dioceses generally approached a limited number of firms whose principals were Catholic and who specialised in this work. The practices of Reynolds & Scott and Weightman & Bullen were especially prominent in the field, the former producing broadly conservative designs, the latter adopting a more modern approach.

The contrast between the two firms is to be seen in two churches built not more than a couple of years apart, Corpus Christi, Halton (1962) and St Nicholas, Gipton (1960–1). The former, by Reynolds & Scott, was built not for the diocese but for the Oblates of Mary Immaculate, a French order, who had built the great Victorian church of Mount St Mary. Corpus Christi forms part of a campus including primary and secondary schools and is planned on a grand scale. In style,

The dramatic east window with its giant cross is the dominant motif of St David, Waincliffe, seen here soon after its construction in 1961. (Kitson Archive)

The interior of Corpus Christi, Halton (1962, Reynolds & Scott) is faced with a rich variety of marbles and is a striking example of how tradition informed much Roman Catholic church design well into the 1960s. [DP029134]

it is broadly Classical, with a broad portico in Hollington stone including paired Ionic columns, although there are elements, particularly in the 27.5m-high tower, of Romanesque. Its cathedral-like interior with a great barrel-vaulted roof draws on Byzantine inspiration (*opposite*). The plan is that of a basilica with three pairs of transepts intersecting the aisles. Side chapels to Our Lady and St Joseph are separated from the chancel by columns of green marble with Carrara marble capitals. The chapels are lined in marble and gold mosaic, and the east end of the church as a whole is sumptuously decorated in a variety of different marbles. At the west end a baroque organ case in white and gold flanks the west window, whose stained glass shows a copy of Murillo's *Assumption of Our Lady*. It is hard to believe the date of the church, as it is in the style of 30 years earlier, and the building is an exceptional contribution to an area of Leeds that lacks landmarks.

Weightman & Bullen's St Nicholas is undeniably a church for the 1960s, the first Catholic church to move decisively away from traditional brick idioms to steel, concrete and glass. It resembles other churches by

Angular forms reflect church design for a new age in St Nicholas, Gipton (1960–1, Weightman & Bullen). [DP027125]

this practice, most notably in the design of the slender 21m pierced tower over the baptistery. The pronounced vertical emphasis is heightened by the closely spaced vertical glazing bars of the generous nave glazing and by a second 9m-high tower over the sanctuary, recalling that of Gillespie, Kidd & Coia's St Paul's at Glenrothes, Fife (1957), which provides concealed light to the altar. A folded fibrous plaster ceiling, originally painted gold and white, combines with mosaic on the east wall, abstract glass in the west window and chiselled coloured glass by Pierre Fourmaintreaux of Whitefriars Studio to give a punchy, energetic feel to the church. Dating from just before the Second Vatican Council of 1962–5 (with its insistence on the involvement of the laity in the mass), its high altar was placed against the east wall, although the ceiling rose towards the sanctuary to make the nave seem shorter so as to more fully engage the congregation in the performance of the mass.

New directions

At the same time, the Church of England was exploring new directions in worship. One, the House Church movement, was associated with the Reverend Ernie Southcott, vicar of St Wilfrid, Halton. For Southcott, the building was not synonymous with the church and he instigated meetings and communion in people's houses as a way of ministering to those who would not otherwise attend services in a church. Halton achieved national fame in the 1950s, but the concept failed to survive Southcott's move from the parish. The Anglicans were also seeking a more radical approach to church design. Geoffrey Davy of the firm of Kitson, Parish, Ledgard & Pyman (later Kitson, Pyman & Partners) had already designed two relatively conventional churches, one Anglican, St Stephen, Moor Allerton (1954), which was a hall church, and St Andrew, Old Lane, Beeston (1956) for the Methodists. He visited Le Corbusier's celebrated chapel at Ronchamp and developed an interest in liturgical planning, joining the influential New Churches Research Group, founded by the Reverend Peter Hammond, author of *Liturgy and Architecture* (1960), and the architect Robert Maguire. The three churches that Davy built in otherwise unremarkable suburbs between 1959 and 1965 display a fascination with a plan whose object is to ensure that nothing stands

Geoffrey Davy designed three churches that are the most innovative Anglican churches of the mid-20th century in Leeds. Their plans evince a desire to experiment and to ensure that nothing came between the priest and his congregation. St Paul, Raynel Drive, Ireland Wood (1964-5) (below), St David, Waincliffe (1961) (right, top), St Cyprian with St James, Harehills (1958–9) (right, bottom). (Redrawn by George Wilson from original plans from the Kitson Archive).

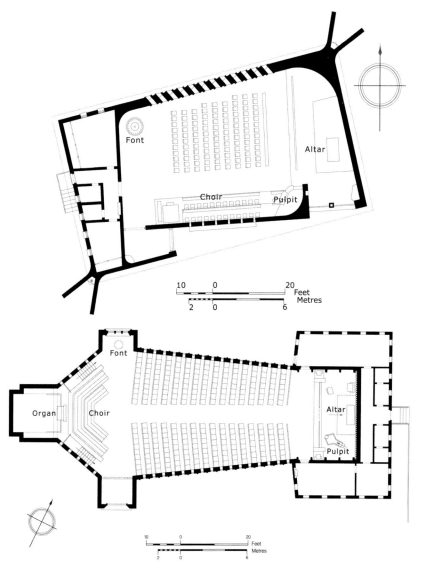

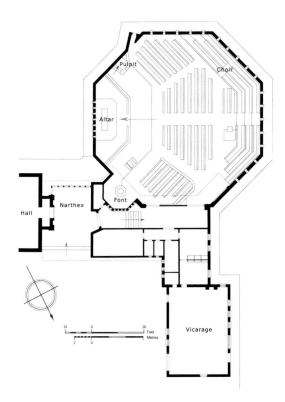

between the priest and his congregation, a willingness to exploit the decorative possibilities of brick and the development of a personal style. They show what a provincial architect, enthused by new architectural currents, could achieve on a limited budget.

St Cyprian with St James showing the nave splayed towards the sanctuary. [DP020914]

The first of the churches replaced a temporary building in an Edwardian area. St Cyprian with St James, Coldcotes Avenue, Harehills (1958–9) is designed around an organ from the city centre church of St James, placed at the west end in the centre of a canted west wall, while the nave walls are splayed inwards towards the east end. Davy had firmly held views that there should be no barrier between priest and people, and the choir stalls are placed at the west end. Other elements of Davy's design that were repeated in his other churches are the tall slit-like windows filled with Belgian-made 'antique' glass, some coloured in abstract patterns, the exposed brick of the walls and the varnished deal boarding of the ceiling. The Corbusian influence is most apparent in the small rectangular windows punched into the west wall, filled with coloured glass.

St David, Dewsbury Road, Waincliffe (1960–1) is designed to be viewed from the main Dewsbury Road, with its striking south elevation catching the eye of the motorist heading south out of the city. Its plan is a rectangle but the south wall is angled inwards and the interior follows this axis, setting up a powerful tension between interior and exterior and making what is essentially a small and simple building a spatially complex one. The dominant themes of the interior are the great sweep of the hyperbolic paraboloid roof and the curve of the sanctuary wall that meets it, a curve echoed in the sharper radius of the projecting wall behind the pulpit. A full-height window behind the pulpit pours light across the sanctuary from a hidden source, and the roof rises from the entrance to reach its highest point here (*see* p 36). The refined simplicity of St David's recalls that of Basil Spence's contemporary work in Coventry and Sheffield.

For the final church in the series, St Paul, Raynel Drive, Ireland Wood (1964–5), Davy had to link the new building to the existing hall church of 1951, which became the church hall. He deliberated on the shape of the church, settling on an octagon, which retained the strength of a circular building but also allowed the eye to focus on the altar and east window placed on the periphery. The entry route to the church is equally carefully considered: a low-key entrance gives restricted views of the interior but reveals the font, marking baptism as entry into the church. As with its two predecessors, St Paul's owes a great deal to the detailed design work by Charles Sewell, Davy's senior assistant. All three churches have fittings and furniture designed by the architect, their simplicity echoing that of the European examples featured in *Liturgy and Architecture*. The most striking are the tubular steel cross and light fittings at St Paul's (described by the architects as 'harsh and uncompromising').

As time went on, the Leeds Catholics too became much more adventurous. Derek Walker carried out reconstructions of the sanctuaries of two churches. In 1959, he transformed Our Lady of Lourdes, Cardigan Road (1930) with successive rows of screens supported on a steel framework into which relief modelling of angels' faces by Jill Messenger were inserted. Illuminated stained glass by Roy Lewis was placed in front of the screens. Above, a metal grid of small light bulbs symbolising the Crown of Thorns serves as a baldacchino. The following year, Walker remodelled St Augustine, Harehills (*see* p 20 and p 26) with stainless steel altar rails (since removed), a mosaic of the Risen Christ and a baldacchino. That there were limits to the acceptance of modernism is evident from the bishop's vetoing a gesso painting by Tom Watt of the Crucifixion and sculpture by Jill Messenger.

Walker went on to build two churches for the diocese, one on the city's edge at Garforth (St Benedict, demolished) and the other the Church of the Sacred Heart, Woodsley Road (1963–5) – now the Leeds Grand Mosque (*see* p 63) – which replaced a 19th-century building in a part of Hyde Park that was redeveloped. It is a brutalist design with a concrete frame clad in pre-cast concrete Cornish granite aggregate panels. This harsh exterior was relieved at the west end by a large glazed box-like baptistery that injected light into the building. The 23m span across the nave enabled its length to be compressed, giving the congregation much greater intimacy with the performance of the mass, and the choir was on a gallery at the west end for the same reason. The nave was lit by a north-light roof, the sanctuary by high-level lights above it. Prominent are the paired concrete beams, which alternate with brick infill in the interior and enclose tall slit-like windows.

A dull church had its sanctuary transformed by Derek Walker (who became the chief planner of Milton Keynes and the architect of the Leeds Armouries in later years) in 1959. Our Lady of Lourdes, Cardigan Road, has screens with stained glass by Roy Lewis. [DP028563]

A practical approach

These churches, however, were the exceptions. The remaining Anglican and Catholic churches of the late 1950s and 1960s, although a vast improvement to the temporary huts they so often replaced, were architecturally less distinctive. It was, though, one of the most sustained programmes of church building since before the First World War. Most were small and designed by local firms of architects. The favoured style was that broadly described as neo-Scandinavian: low-pitched roofs spanning brick walls with large windows, often with a linked hall. What was common to many of them was a lack of a sense of mystery, perhaps appropriate in a more secular age. Most served housing estates, both private and council, and in a sense this apparent blandness meant that they actually fitted their surroundings well in that they shared many of their materials and their style (or the lack of any powerful expression of it) with the houses they served and were not the visual focus of a community in the way that their grand Victorian predecessors were.

Those built on council estates were given more prominent sites than those serving private housing. In the latter category are St Barnabas, The View, Alwoodley (1963), with a low bell tower, and Holy Trinity, Green Lane, Cookridge (1961–2, Jones, Stocks & Partners), with a canted east end and tall south-east tower. St Barnabas is at the end of a cul-de-sac and Holy Trinity is on a secondary road, and these settings contrast with those such as the Ascension, Foundry Mill Street (1961) and St Richard, Ramshead Hill (designed 1955, opened 1961) on the council's Seacroft estate, which are located by the junction of several roads. St Richard, by Jones & Stocks, has tall windows, grouped in threes with concrete mullions, intended to be linked with a hall for which the funds never materialised.

Much the same comments could be made about the nonconformist churches of the period. Those at Cookridge (1962, W F Dawson & Bennett) and Sandford (1960) are typical of the practical approach generally employed. Only Headingley St Columba (*see* front cover), built on a sloping site in 1966 for the Presbyterians, stands out with its generous glazing, peaked roofs, and meeting rooms raised on concrete columns.

St Richard, Seacroft (1955, Jones & Stocks) is typical of many of the churches built on the housing estates in the 1950s where the architect had to work within a limited budget. [DP020920]

7

Coming full circle: 1960s to the present

Redevelopment and the construction of new roads and motorways had a massive impact on places of worship in Leeds from the mid-1960s. A process that had begun between the wars in Hunslet and Holbeck, in the east end and the Leylands reached its climax in these years. The routeing of the extension of the M1 motorway across the south side of the city, cutting off Beeston from the centre, created social divisions and planning blight and led to the area enclosed by the motorway being largely rebuilt with a much lower population density (*see* map, p 4). The old inner districts, the heart of Leeds Methodism, lost any coherence they once had; the main roads into the centre, once lined with shops, pubs and chapels, became feeders to the new road system, which imposed a cordon sanitaire around a vibrant city centre. The widening of the York Road and the building of the inner ring road tightly across the north side of the city did the same to Burmantofts and Sheepscar. Congregations became separated from the churches that served them. Nonconformist chapels, heavily concentrated in these inner areas, suffered disproportionately from closures and the loss of their congregations.

Only five Anglican churches have been constructed since the 1960s. Instead, the emphasis has been on altering existing buildings to suit present-day needs. In a number of cases, including Christ Church, Upper Armley, St Cross, Middleton (*see* p 25) and St Wilfrid, Harehills, the naves have been subdivided to provide a parish hall in the rear part of the building.

All Hallows, Regent Terrace, by Castelow & Partners, which stands on top of a hill in the redeveloped part of Hyde Park, replaced Kelly & Birchall's church of 1886, which was destroyed by fire in 1970. It is an irregularly shaped building with a large, sparsely furnished worship space that has had a café added, which provides community facilities. What distinguishes the interior is the stained-glass east window of the Risen Christ by Frank Roper, who also designed the three light fittings (*overleaf*). Roper, who carried out important commissions at Durham, St David's and Peterborough cathedrals, was also responsible for the stained glass at St Mary, Hunslet as well as the extraordinary canopy, a little like the underside of a mushroom, that sweeps down from the centre of the roof of the church to terminate in a cast-aluminium sculpture,

One of Jerzy Faczynski's striking Stations of the Cross at St Gregory the Great, Swarcliffe (1969–70), executed in black line on coloured glass. [DP027709]

Frank Roper's stylish light fittings at All Hallows, Regent Terrace incorporate texts from the revised Anglican liturgy. [DP028547]

Only the steeple of the Victorian church of St Mary, Hunslet remains; the rest was replaced in 1975 by a new building by Peter Hill. [DP034021]

The Apostles and the People. The centre of Hunslet is entirely redeveloped, with St Mary close to the supermarket that is at the heart of the community today. Only the steeple of the 1862–4 church by Perkin & Backhouse was retained, the remainder replaced in 1975 by a structure built of re-dressed sandstone from its predecessor in a design that owed something to a castle keep, with its heavily rounded corners and slit-like windows to the meeting rooms. The architect was Peter Hill of Hill Mawson Partnership, who also rebuilt All Saints, York Road in 1980. St Peter, Hunslet Moor, a box-like structure of the 1970s with nothing but its name prominently displayed on its eaves to denote its function, marks the ultimate move away from the traditional image of a church.

The Stations of the Cross at St Gregory the Great, Swarcliffe (1969–70, L A G Pritchard Son & Partners) take the novel form of coloured glass with black line drawings by Jerzy Faczynski in small windows that punctuate the west wall, with all the Stations set out in one place rather than being spread around the church. [DP027707]

The Second Vatican Council and the resulting changes in the liturgy made their first major impact on Catholic churches in Leeds with the building of St Gregory the Great (1969–70, L A G Pritchard Son & Partners), on a postwar housing estate in Swarcliffe. The church is dominated by striking stained glass by Adam Kossowski and distinguished externally by a hyperbolic paraboloid roof. The Second Vatican Council's effects on church design in Leeds reached their apogee in St Joseph, Hunslet (J H Langtry-Langton) in 1971. This was a centrally planned church, taking much of its inspiration, like many Catholic churches of the period, from Sir Frederick Gibberd's Liverpool Cathedral. Located in an area that has undergone vast change since its

construction, it was closed in 1994 because of continual vandalism and demolished in 2005. Our Lady of Czestochowa and St Stanislau by John Brunton & Partners (1976) serves Leeds' Polish community, which settled like so many others in the large and adaptable houses of Chapeltown.

Subsequent churches have continued the emphasis on the active participation of the laity in the mass and have the congregation arranged in a semicircle around the communion table so that no-one's view of the sanctuary is obstructed and all are accommodated as closely to it as is possible. The buildings are, however, much less radical than St Joseph. St Francis of Assisi, Beeston Hill (1984, J H Langtry-Langton & Partners) was the first of three churches to be built in a red-brick style whose cosy domesticity, with warm red brick and pitched hipped roofs, reflects the suburban setting in which it stands. St Paul, King Lane (Jos Townend of Edwin Trotter Associates, 1996) and two churches by

St Patrick, Torre Road, Burmantofts (2001, Michael Bateson Associates) follows current Roman Catholic practice with both the church and rooms for social functions contained under one roof. [DP034013]

Michael Bateson Associates – St Philip, Middleton (1996, replacing the church brought from the city centre, demolished for structural reasons) and St Patrick, Torre Road, Burmantofts (2001) – are the latest examples of the style, the first two sharing their sites with primary schools. All three are replacements of existing churches and have a degree of anonymity, lacking traditional architectural elements such as a tower to proclaim their purpose and relying on prominent crosses to make clear their function (*opposite*). Inside, a conscious attempt has been made to make them warm and welcoming, with seating placed in a U-shape around the altar. The worship space thus gains a degree of intimacy, bringing the congregation together and involving them in the mass, in a manner difficult to achieve in a church designed on traditional lines.

The 1970s and 1980s saw the trend established in the 1960s – of building new Methodist chapels to replace large Victorian structures – gathering pace. Like their predecessors, many were simple utilitarian buildings but some are much more ambitious, with significant attempts to provide a variety of community facilities. Hyde Park Methodist Mission (1976) by Brooks Thorp Partners replaced four 19th-century Methodist churches with a complex that includes a worship space taking the shape of a cube with cut-off corners, a coffee bar and a large hall with several interlinked side rooms, all approached through a central common entrance. The top-lit worship space is the tallest element in the composition and stands out clearly within it. But subsequent Methodist churches have concentrated all their activities under a single roof, so that the part set aside for worship is no longer externally expressed in an obvious way. Hunslet Methodist Church (1981, Hill Mawson) and Christ Church, Halton (1992, J H Langtry-Langton), which is shared by the Methodists and the United Reformed Church, exemplify this trend.

There are many independent evangelical, Pentecostal and charismatic churches in the Leeds suburbs. Their buildings tend to be unadorned brick halls, such as the premises of the Tinshill Free Church, Bramley Christian Church and West Grange Church, a style also favoured by the Church of the Nazarene at Grove Road, Hunslet and at Hunslet Hall Road and by the Jehovah's Witnesses in their Kingdom Halls in Hunslet, Halton and Stainbeck Lane. Purpose-built rather than reused buildings are favoured, although a notable exception is the church of the Woodhouse Christian Fellowship in Holborn Approach, the 1850 former premises of a Temperance Hall and Mechanics Institute (in appearance somewhat like a chapel with a gable facing the road), founded by Samuel Smiles.

New immigrants

From the 1950s to the 1970s, many Afro-Caribbean people, principally from Jamaica, St Kitts and Nevis, and Barbados, moved to Leeds, initially settling in Chapeltown, and the black majority churches have been among the fastest growing in the city. Music and the active participation of the congregation play an important role, and while the internal form of the churches generally resembles that of the nonconformists, space for choirs and a band is usually provided. Another feature of Pentecostal worship is the absence of images of Christ, biblical texts often providing the sole decoration. One of the largest churches is the New Testament Church of God (*opposite*), which occupies the former Third Church of Christ Scientist, Easterly Road, Harehills (1927) by Davidson, Son & Sherwood. The church was established in Leeds in 1959 and initially met in private homes before moving to the former Congregational church behind the Union Chapel in Chapeltown Road, premises also used at different times by the Jewish and Hindu communities. The move to Easterly Road came in 1984. The large neo-Georgian church has required few changes to suit its new role; additional choir stalls were added for the church's two gospel choirs, and a mixing desk for sound and lighting was installed at the rear. The First United Church of Jesus Christ is located in W S Braithwaite's robustly Gothic United Methodist Free Church, Victoria Road, Hyde Park (1886). Another example of reuse is the Church of Jesus Christ Apostolic, part of a US-based Pentecostal church with nine churches in Great Britain, which bought the former Church of Christ (1900) in Gledhow Road in the early 1980s. Three other groups also use this church: a French-speaking Congolese church, the Eritrean Brethren and a Ugandan congregation. The last 10 years have seen increasing numbers of Africans fleeing oppression in their own countries, and this is reflected in the rise of African churches whose services are held in languages other than English. None of these churches has obtained its own premises as

The broad nave of the New Testament Church of God, built as a Christian Science church in the 1920s (Davidson, Son & Sherwood), is well suited to the large congregation. Note the emphasis on the Word and the absence of images of Christ – both characteristic features of Pentecostal worship. [IMG 2169]

yet, and they use other denominations' churches or community facilities. There are at least 14 such churches meeting in the Harehills and Chapeltown area alone. Again this is not a new phenomenon: the Chinese Christians have met for some years at Hyde Park Methodist Mission.

Two black majority churches in Chapeltown constructed new buildings in 1982. In Laycock Place the Wesleyan Holiness Church built a simple brick building, surrounded by the high-security fencing that reflects the defensive nature of much inner-city architecture today, while the Church of God of Prophecy opened their new building on Chapeltown Road next to the Sikh Temple. The church had been established in Leeds for some 40 years and formerly occupied the Baptist chapel in Meanwood Road (1881, Smith & Tweedale). The church is unusual in that its worship space is also used as a community hall, which attracted public funding. Consequently, no Christian symbols are displayed within it, as it is felt these would be inappropriate when it is used for secular purposes and that the congregation has no need for such visual evidence of faith. The building is highly flexible in layout, having a movable rostrum and sliding doors opening onto a space that can accommodate an overflow congregation.

New synagogues

The Jewish population had been moving steadily northwards since the 1930s, and as Leeds Jewry was largely Orthodox, this led to increasing difficulty in maintaining older places of worship, because of Orthodox prohibitions on travel on the Sabbath. The area favoured was Moortown, where a synagogue was established in the former United Methodist Free Church and where an outpost of the large Beth Hamedrash Hagadol synagogue, which was located at Back Nile Street, the Leylands, was opened in a prefabricated building in the late 1950s.

The first of the new purpose-built synagogues to be erected was the Sinai Reform Synagogue (1960, Halpern & Associates), which had moved from the former Spanish and Portuguese Synagogue in Chapeltown. The only Reform synagogue in the city, it was almost doubled in size with the addition of the shul to the east side of the building in 1984–5. Somewhat industrial in appearance, it is distinguished by its treatment of the east

United Hebrew Congregation Synagogue (1985–6, P Langtry-Langton) has a striking design built around the fine stained-glass windows that came from the Great Synagogue. [DP034040]

windows, which, with contrasting brickwork, form the shape of a menorah (a seven-branched candelabra that symbolises Judaism). The largest of the synagogues is Beth Hamedrash Hagadol, which replaced a prefabricated building with what is reputed to be the largest synagogue outside London. Seating 1100, it was designed by G Alan Burnett and has a glazed lantern as the centre of a Star of David formed by the deep exposed roof beams. Externally, a band of glazing at the level of the eaves runs continuously around the shul.

The two other synagogues are located north of the ring road. Etz Chaim (1980–1, Stuart Leventhal of Owen Diplock & Associates) was built in brown brick, and its blocky, largely windowless forms contrast greatly with the United Hebrew Congregation's decidedly retro design commissioned from Peter Langtry-Langton in 1985–6 (*opposite*). This incorporated parts of the bimah (centrally positioned reading desk) from the New Synagogue in Chapeltown and the pulpit from the Great Synagogue in Belgrave Street, the building itself being designed around the stained-glass windows removed from its two predecessors. What unites all three of the Orthodox synagogues is their use of a hexagonal shul, although they otherwise vary greatly in internal design in such matters as the placement of the women's gallery, which is on the same level at the United Hebrew Congregation and raised in the traditional manner at the other two. The United Hebrew Congregation is prominently located on Shadwell Lane, Sinai is on a residential road and the other two have no real street frontages at all, with Beth Hamedrash down a drive and Etz Chaim screened by trees from the Harrogate Road.

It is arguable whether a congregation needs a permanent building at all today. Some of the fast-growing evangelical churches that have succeeded in attracting younger people meet in city-centre hotels, while there is a reversion to the age-old practice of meeting in people's homes in the practice of church seeding. In this sense, perhaps, the wheel has gone full circle, with echoes of 18th-century nonconformists meeting in private homes before they acquired the funds to build a chapel or of Ernie Southcott's belief that you could take the church to the people rather than wait in vain for them to come to church.

8

Faiths established in Leeds since 1945

As will have become clear in the preceding chapters, the story of faith in Leeds is one of constant movement, of newcomers moving to the city, settling close to the centre and then gradually moving outwards towards the suburbs. It happened with the Irish Catholic, the Jewish and the Polish Catholic communities. The story is repeated with all those who have come to live in Leeds since the Second World War. The difference is that the process has speeded up, so that what may have taken many generations to achieve is now accomplished in one or two. This has a considerable impact on religious buildings in that the congregations of places of worship may eventually live far from the premises serving them. The fear has been expressed that all the effort and expense in creating a fine building may be wasted if it turns out to be a white elephant when its congregation has moved on geographically.

The Sikhs

The Sikh community were the first Asians in Leeds to organise religious worship, first meeting together in a private house in 1953. Soon after, they regularly began performing kirtan (singing of religious scriptures from the *Sri Guru Granth Sahib*, the holy book of Sikhism) at a house in Clarendon Road, near the city centre. In 1957, the first Sikh temple in Yorkshire was opened in a converted terraced house at 3 Savile Road, Potternewton. The former Newton Park Union Chapel, Chapeltown Road (*overleaf*), was acquired in 1960 and remained in use as the gurdwara (place of worship) until 1999, when the present gurdwara was opened opposite it.

The present gurdwara by Singh & Partners is a boxy steel-framed building that incorporates a traditional dome above the central part of the façade, which extends to form a porte-cochère. Octagonal turrets topped by small onion domes mark the corners of the building. It has a diwan (worship room) on the first floor, a large kitchen and dining area on the ground floor for the serving of langar (the meal that is an integral part of Sikh worship) and a further large hall in the basement. The traditional Sikh flag pole stands outside the building. Adjacent to the building, a Sikh centre for social events and meetings has been built, while the former premises in the Union Chapel have been refurbished to provide

The Sikh Temple on Chapeltown Road (1999, Singh & Partners) displays a flagpole, an important symbol of the Sikh religion. [IMG 2537]

accommodation for weddings and events. The Union Chapel is a microcosm of the changing face of religion in Leeds. The earliest part of it (to the rear of the main building) by W H Harris was opened as a Congregational Chapel in 1871. After the building of the new chapel, designed by Archibald Neill, in 1887, it became a hall and was let to serve as a synagogue and a meeting place for Hindus and Jains before being incorporated into the Sikh Centre. Burnt out in 2003, the shell may be refurbished as part of the overall restoration of what is one of the most exciting religious buildings in Leeds. The Union Chapel, originally shared by the Baptists and the Congregationalists, has a centrally planned nave and an extraordinarily complex roof, while the exterior has a half-octagonal porch and flying buttresses, rather in the manner of a 'rogue' architect such as E B Lamb and all thrown together with tremendous gusto. The partitions that had subdivided the building have been taken out and the great open space of the nave can be seen again.

Chapeltown is a centre for the Sikh community, although most live on the northern outskirts of the city. Two further small gurdwaras have been converted from large private houses, the Gurdwara Kalgidhar Sahib Bhatra Sangat in a stone villa on Chapeltown Road and the Gurdwara Nanhari Sangat in an early 19th-century red-brick Classical house in Louis Street. Much more substantial is the Ramgarhia Sikh Centre, a little to the south in Sheepscar, where a large multipurpose complex of brick-built halls owing nothing to traditional design opened in 1987. It includes a sports hall, squash court and a day centre for the elderly. Its large car park, a feature shared with the Chapeltown Road gurdwara, reflects the fact that few if any of its members now live locally.

The other two gurdwaras in Leeds have both reused existing buildings. The Guru Nanak Sikh Gurdwara, Tong Road, New Wortley occupies the former Mount Pisgah United Methodist Free Church of 1877, a handsome Italianate chapel and its adjacent schools. It was established there in 1978 and, unlike Chapeltown, most of the congregation live locally in the Armley area. A need for a temple for Sikhs living on the south side of Leeds prompted the opening of the Gurdwara Gurunanak Nishkam Sewak Jatha in Lady Pit Lane, Hunslet. This, opened in 1987, was converted from the former Rington's tea factory of

The Sikh gurdwara was until 1999 housed in the former Newton Park Union Chapel (1887, Archibald Neil), which has been converted to function rooms and a hall for the Sikh community. [IMG 2178]

The former Ringston's tea factory in Hunslet provides ample space for the many community facilities incorporated at Gurdwara Gurunanak Nishkam Sewak Jatha. [DP029100]

1936, a large and impressive three-storey building. All the conversion work was undertaken by the community and is still continuing as parts of the building are brought into use. The open areas of the factory floors have been partitioned to provide two diwans on the first and second floors, with the kitchen and dining room on the ground floor. As with the other large gurdwaras, extensive facilities have been provided, including a photographic studio, computer room and space for traditional Sikh activities such as martial arts and archery, the archery range being located in the hayloft of a late 19th-century stable incorporated into the factory.

Hindu temples

The Hindu Charitable Trust was formed in 1968. Two years later it purchased a large Victorian house in Alexandra Road from the Salvation Army. Used initially as a temple, it is now a community centre after the opening of the Shree Hindu Mandir (2001–2), designed by Rajesh Sompura, an architect practising in India. This temple intriguingly blends West Riding stone vernacular with Indian temple architecture. Built in the grounds of the original temple, it incorporates an existing building on the site, probably a former stable. The mandir has an intricate mandapa (porch), carved in India, and the buttresses on the end walls terminate in chattri (small domed towers) of traditional Indian design. Inside, the temple is quite plain, and the emphasis is placed on the marble shrines containing the deities against the west wall. These introduce colour into the building, echoed in the large paintings of deities on the wall opposite them. The combination of East and West is especially striking in the building, which draws upon both traditions to fit into its setting within 'the Harolds', a tightly built-up toast rack of back-to-back houses in Hyde Park. Again, like the Sikhs, few of the members still live in the area, and a large car park is provided.

Mosques

The faith community whose places of worship have had the greatest visual impact on Leeds in recent years are the Muslims, with five purpose-built mosques constructed within the last 10 years, four of them of considerable size. Like the faiths already mentioned, the Muslims started with meetings in converted houses, the first being the Jinnah Mosque, 21 Leopold Street, Chapeltown, opened in 1961 in a house formerly used as a synagogue. Most Muslims in Leeds came from Pakistan, Bangladesh and India, but within the last 10 years they have been joined by others from Middle Eastern countries and North Africa and by those seeking asylum from war-torn regions such as Bosnia and Chechnya. In addition, there has been an increase in overseas students, particularly from the Middle East. While prayers and matters relating to the Koran are invariably read in Arabic, sermons are given in the language of the majority of the congregation. This has led to the creation

The traditional porch of the Shree Hindu Mandir was carved in India and designed by Rajesh Sompura, an architect practising there. [DP034134]

of new mosques serving different parts of the Muslim community that share the essential requirements for Muslim worship: a large prayer hall, a niche (mihrab) indicating the direction of Mecca and forming the focus of prayer, and washing facilities (wudu).

Examples of mosques in an embryo stage are those based in terraced houses in Beeston Hill: the Muslim Association Mosque and Madrasa, Stratford Street, and the Shahkamal Jamra Masjid and Madrasa in Rowland Terrace. Conversions include that from the Leeds Industrial Co-Operative Society's Beeston Hill branch of 1893 in Hardy Street, now the Kashmir Muslim Community Centre and Mosque (*see* p 2); the Quba Mosque, Hares Avenue, Harehills, converted from a garage; the Bilal Mosque, Harehills Place, formerly the Sunday School (1891) of Harehills Congregational Church; and the Makki Masjid and Madrasa in Vicarage Road, Hyde Park, built in the 1970s as the church hall of All Hallows Church.

Much the most impressive conversion is that of the former Roman Catholic Church of the Sacred Heart, Woodsley Road, Hyde Park into

*Bilal Mosque stands prominently on Harehills Lane and its visual dominance becomes clear when it is compared with the other places of worship in the area; the former Harehills Congregational Church (1900-01, Tom Dyer), on Harehills Road at top right and to its right the Roman Catholic Church of St Augustine of Canterbury (1937, Gribbon, Foggitt & Brown), itself a sizeable building (*above, left*). [NMR 20666/028 24-AUG-2007 © English Heritage.NMR]*

*The Makkah Mosque towers over the surrounding back-to-back terraces in exactly the same way as Temple Moore's great church of St Margaret of Antioch (1908-9) does – both have enormous townscape value in punctuating the otherwise uniform rows of two and three-storey terraces and contributing to a sense of place (*above, right*). [NMR 20666/043 24-AUG-2007 © English Heritage.NMR]*

the Leeds Grand Mosque, which uses Arabic and English for sermons and discussion. The former church, described on p 44, remains little altered externally, other than the modification of the roof over what was the east end, which was leaking. Two wings either side of the former baptistery provide toilet and wudu facilities. The former nave has been reoriented so that the mihrab is located in the centre of what was liturgically the south wall. The former chancel has been partitioned off with a glass and uPVC (unplasticised PVC) screen to form a second smaller worship hall used during weekdays. The former chapels either side of it now house the administrator's office. Women play an important role in Leeds Grand Mosque, and the existing women's gallery raised up behind a uPVC screen at what is now the rear of the worship area, which was not large enough, has been augmented by a second gallery, added by enclosing the former choir gallery. While the furnishings were stripped when the church was deconsecrated, some Christian symbolism remains in the crosses in the striking handles to the steel doors to the building.

One of the most striking churches to be built in the 1960s was Derek Walker's Church of the Sacred Heart (1963–5), now Leeds Grand Mosque. This view of the interior shows the carpet marked out for prayers, with the mihrab (the niche indicating the direction of Mecca) and the minbar (pulpit) in the centre and the former choir above the doors that is now screened off as a women's gallery. [DP 034006]

The first of the new breed of purpose-built mosques to go up was the Jamia Masjid Gohsia in Brooklyn Terrace, Armley, built in 1996. It is also the smallest of them and was built in two phases. The earlier part is a brick single-storey hall with hipped roof akin to a community centre in appearance with nothing to distinguish it as a mosque. It was later extended at the front to provide the traditional elements of a dome, two small minarets and a pointed arch over the entrance. It serves Armley's Pakistani Sunni community.

Al-Samarraie's Makkah Masjid (2003) dominates the surrounding streets of Hyde Park in much the same way as a Victorian Gothic church would have done. [DP028565]

The second to be built makes much more of a visual impact on the city. Constructed in 1999, the Bilal Mosque (*see* frontispiece and p 62) is sited on the side of a hill off the busy Harehills Lane and can be seen towering above the terraced streets below from across the city. It is the largest mosque in the city and was designed by Atba Al-Samarraie, a prominent designer of mosques and Islamic schools, whose firm Archi-Structure, based in Baildon, West Yorkshire, has designed three of the city's five purpose-built mosques. Built of blockwork, it displays the shaped gables seen in his other mosques, together with tall octagonal minarets on each corner of the symmetrical entrance façade and pointed window heads. Al-Samarraie was also involved in the Makkah Masjid, Brudenell Road, Hyde Park, opened in 2003 (*opposite*). This too dominates the local landscape in the way that a great High Anglican church would have done in the 19th century, its green dome and minarets forming a landmark above the terraces. It was built on the site of a former independent (later Christadelphian) timber chapel that was in poor repair and lacked an alternative use. The group, which had its origins in the early 1970s, raised £1.5 million within the local community. In style it is, like Harehills Lane, a mix of traditional Islamic elements but combined here with a neo-Victorian sensibility that enables it to fit well into its surroundings. The walls are of cream brick with bright red-brick bands, supplying a polychromatic effect worthy of William Butterfield. Particularly impressive is the portico facing Thornville Road, which has four tall thin columns of cream brick cut in a barley sugar pattern. The plan of the building is quite simple, with a large prayer hall on each floor and a smaller subsidiary hall on the first and second floors. Women have their own entrance leading directly to a prayer hall in the lower ground floor. The dome is open and lights the upper prayer hall. Both Harehills Lane and Makkah Mosque have sermons in Urdu.

Shah Jalal Mosque, Ellers Road, Harehills, the third mosque to be designed by Al-Samarraie, is smaller but, if anything, is even more successful in the way in which it engages with the Victorian red-brick terraces of the surrounding area (*see* p 67). The Bangladesh Islamic Society was formed in 1978 and converted two houses in Ellers Road into a mosque. Expansion was needed to meet the needs of the area's growing Bangladeshi population, and the existing houses were demolished and replaced in 2003–4 by the purpose-built mosque, which cost around £800,000, all the funds being raised within the local Bangladeshi community. It is located on a corner site and picks up the rhythm of the gables of the houses in the street. Its minaret is positioned at the corner and marks it in a very satisfying way. The building seems 'right' in its position as a focal point for the area in the way a nonconformist chapel might once have done, and the analogy is continued by the neat plaque bearing the mosque's name in incised lettering much as one would once have read the words 'Zion' or 'Moriah'. Inside, the mosque follows the usual pattern, although the mihrab is more ornate and the minbar (pulpit) is also of an elaborate design. The mosque also differs in that no provision is made for women.

Also in Harehills is the Central Jamia Mosque, also known as the Leeds Islamic Centre, in Spencer Place. Designed by Finn & Downes Associates and built in 1997–2000, it replaced the former Chadssidishe Shul synagogue of 1934, which remains in use as a hall behind the new mosque. It has a steel frame, clad in polychrome brick, a large central dome, twin minarets and rounded staircase towers on each corner, giving it something of the appearance of a castle keep. The mihrab is expressed externally by a rounded projection in the centre of the east wall, which is punctuated by tall arched openings. Sermons are in Urdu.

What stands out in the expansion of the Muslim, Hindu and Sikh communities in Leeds is how it exhibits such strong continuities with the past. It echoes what had happened in all Christian denominations. Many Leeds churches had their origins in timber huts or tin tabernacles, while others met in rooms above pubs, and St Gregory, Swarcliffe, was notably housed initially in the priest's council house, with the serving hatch used for confessions! A clear pattern is discernible whereby religious groups initially meet in private houses and then raise the money to purchase one for dedicated use. The group grows and outgrows the converted house and seeks other premises, perhaps reusing a building formerly occupied by a different faith or that was used for secular purposes. Then, when funds are available, a purpose-built structure is commissioned, employing all the traditional architectural features of the faith and incorporating extensive facilities for the community.

Shah Jalal Mosque (2003–4, Atba Al-Samarraie) picks up the rhythm of the surrounding Victorian terraces and relates well to them – very much in the Leeds tradition. [DP034019]

9

Places of worship
in Leeds: the future

Trevor Mitchell

The long process of housing clearance and redevelopment of the inner areas caused profound changes to places of worship in Leeds. The congregations of some churches simply vanished, while others were rehoused some distance from their building. The M1 extension in particular cut off buildings from large parts of their congregations. When this is coupled with the national decline in numbers of those attending services of the established faiths, the problem in terms of historic buildings is clear: Christian church attendance is falling by 2.3 per cent a year in England, a decline of 15 per cent in the last seven years. Added to this, there is little doubt that, as in many cities, Leeds had an over-provision of churches. The factionalism of the Methodist denomination in particular had led to the building of far too many chapels, and these had already started to decline substantially in numbers after the amalgamation of the different branches in 1932.

The figures to some extent speak for themselves (Tables 1 and 2, *overleaf*). In 1905, there were 129 Methodist chapels; in 2006, just 35 of those buildings survive, 22 preserved by alternative uses. The Anglican churches have fared better: 68 (with 29 mission rooms) in 1905, 60 in 2006. But these figures disguise the shift in their location; new churches in the suburbs have replaced those in the inner areas. The vast majority of Leeds' 19th-century chapels have been demolished, mostly since 1945. Many of the most impressive Victorian Anglican churches were located in the inner areas. Losses began in the 1930s and churches by William Butterfield, George Gilbert Scott and G F Bodley disappeared, together with important work by the leading local architects, Thomas Taylor's St Mary, Quarry Hill (1823–5), R D Chantrell's Christ Church, Meadow Lane (1823–5) and George Corson's St Clement, Sheepscar (1868) (*overleaf*). The historic places of worship that survive within the city centre are but a sample of the riches the city once enjoyed. Commercial development and movements in population continue to threaten their futures.

In the early 1980s, the legacy of Victorian places of worship in Leeds became something of a cause célèbre, with many voicing their concern at their continuing demolition. Kenneth Powell, a leading member of the local branch of the Victorian Society, wrote a number of influential

Emmanuel Church, Woodhouse Lane (1880, Adams & Kelly), adapted in 2004 by Halliday Clark to provide accommodation for the University of Leeds chaplaincy. (University of Leeds, EMANOS)

Table 1 Places of worship in Leeds, 1905–2005

	1905	1927	1947	2005
Anglican	68	73	72	60
Anglican mission rooms	29	28	16	–
Roman Catholic	9	12	18	25
Baptist	16	13	12	7
Congregational, Presbyterian, United Reform	22	20	18	8
Methodist	129	116	91	36
Other Christian	35	39	34	39
Jewish	6	11	11	4
Sikh	–	–	–	5
Hindu	–	–	–	1
Muslim	–	–	–	12

Table 2 Dates of construction of churches still in use in Leeds in 2005

	19th century or earlier	1900–1914	1914–1940	1945–2005
Anglican	34	3	8	16
Roman Catholic	1	2	4	17
Baptist	2	–	3	2
Congregational, United Reform	–	2	2	3
Methodist	13	1	2	19

Source: Database of places of worship created for the Religion and Place in Leeds project

reports for the newly established campaigning group SAVE Britain's Heritage. *The Fall of Zion* (1980) highlighted the problem of redundant nonconformist churches with many Leeds examples. In *The New Iconoclasts* (1981) Powell was critical of the management of Anglican buildings in the city. He followed this up with *Churches – A Question of Conversion* (1987) (with Celia De La Hey), which showed how there was a future for such buildings by intelligent conversion to new uses.

The campaign was effective insofar as the last significant demolition, in 1984, was Joseph Botham's magnificent Brunswick Chapel (1824–5) (*opposite page*). The influence of the City Council, Leeds Civic Trust and the Victorian Society in promoting conservation has been important in this change. The denominations themselves have a clearer recognition of the potential of their buildings, evidenced in the approach of the Churches Regional Commission for Yorkshire and the Humber and the moves to create church tourism in the city.

One of the most tragic losses of the 1970s was St Clement, Sheepscar (1868), designed by the important Leeds architect George Corson. The church was on a grand scale in an area that has since been decimated by road schemes. [BB75 05803]

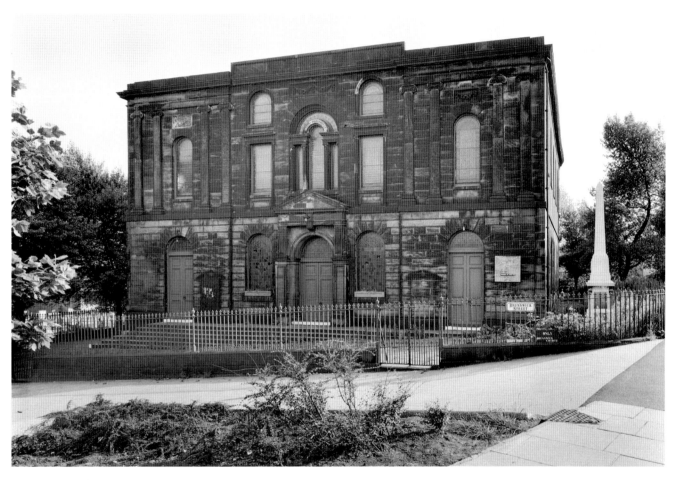

The last significant place of worship to be demolished in Leeds, the Brunswick Chapel (1824–5) by Joseph Botham, pulled down in 1984 despite a long campaign to save it. [BB74 06464]

But the picture is not entirely rosy. Some major former Anglican buildings are currently disused. The city's only surviving church from the two major building campaigns of the early 19th century (the so-called commissioners' churches), St Mark (Peter Atkinson Jnr and R H Sharp, 1823–5), stands empty, awaiting a new use. Some of the former nonconformist chapels present a problem in how to devise an adequate strategy for their conservation. Relatively few survive in anything like their original condition, retaining a full complement of interior fittings such as their galleries, pews, rostrum and organ (*see* p 8). Among these are Seacroft Methodist Church, built in 1821 and refronted in 1874, probably by William Hill, which retains a good interior but is in a parlous condition, Ambler & Bowman's Clowes Primitive Methodist chapel (1893–4), Meanwood Road (now Seventh Day Adventist), which has recently had its galleries restored to use, and the former Gledhow Road Church of Christ (1900, J W Thackray), now Church of Jesus Christ Apostolic, with an unspoilt interior. Some remain with the denomination that built them. Several, such as the former United Methodist Free Church at Armley, are buildings of great character that lift the area in which they are located. Their demolition would be a serious loss both architecturally and historically, given the small number of pre-1914 Methodist chapels, once such a part of the life of the city, that survive (*see* p 74).

The 1874 brick façade (believed to be by William Hill) of the Seacroft Methodist Church hides a much older chapel behind of 1821. Its present condition gives cause for concern. [DP028675]

Seventh Day Adventist Church, Meanwood Road. This restoration of the former Clowes Primitive Methodist chapel (1893–4, Ambler & Bowman) has brought the gallery back into use. [DP034030]

Places of worship are a distinctive building type, providing landmarks on the skyline, serving as the hubs of community identity and providing the local distinctiveness that marks one place out from its neighbour. They are also testaments to the history of faith of a place and its people, even when the original use has ceased. As settings for the ceremonies associated with the key stages of our lives, they have a special significance, even for those who do not regularly attend worship.

But large buildings generate large bills for maintenance and repair. Where existing faith communities cannot afford to keep their buildings going for a few acts of worship on one or two days a week, then new uses are needed to bring income and investment. More intensive use will also

Beeston Methodist Church (1865–6, recently closed) by the prolific local architect William Hill (best known as the architect of Bolton Town Hall) is the epitome of a mid-19th-century Methodist chapel, displaying simple but satisfying detailing of railings and steps. [DP029106]

bring more people into the building, to enjoy its architecture and decoration and to learn about its history. If the interest of the wider community is engaged, then there will be a wider body of friends and supporters who care about the building and will contribute to its upkeep.

Where churches still serve local populations, albeit attracting smaller congregations, compatible new uses can be introduced alongside the continuing religious function. Leeds Parish Church provides meeting spaces and hosts conferences and concerts, as well as providing a café. The Church Institute at St Martin, Potternewton, is home to many community and educational groups. At the Church of the Epiphany, Gipton (*see* pp 28–9), the attached church hall is to be refurbished as a base for Gipton Community Arts Centre. In ways such as these the original role of the church building as a focus for community cohesion, in Edwardian suburbs and postwar estates, can be revived.

New uses often require changes to the building. These should be planned with the aim of retaining the elements that generate the architectural and historical significance of the place. However, there is

Emmanuel Church, Woodhouse Lane (1880, Adams & Kelly) retains the core of its impressive neo-Gothic interior in a conversion to an ecumenical student centre for the University of Leeds. (University of Leeds, EMANOS)

sometimes a need to attract new investment and to signal change, adding a new chapter to the story of a building and its locality. Then it is sometimes necessary to balance the effect on the building's significance against the need to achieve long-term sustainability and wider social and economic benefits for the community. The University of Leeds has taken on two buildings that no longer had viable religious uses – Emmanuel Church, Woodhouse Lane (1880, Adams & Kelly) (*see* p 68 and p 75) and the chapel of the former Leeds Grammar School – introducing new structures to house teaching space and a textile archive.

Government policy guidance on sustainable development and the historic environment (*Delivering Sustainable Development* (Planning Policy Statement 1) 2005 and *Planning and the Historic Environment* (Planning Policy Guidance 15) 1994) recognises that historic buildings add to the quality of our lives by enhancing the local scene and sustaining local character. It urges local councils to put in place policies that will promote and reinforce local distinctiveness. Leeds City Council has ambitious plans to regenerate the mosaic of neighbourhoods that make up the city. Places of worship are often at the hearts of these places, lending a distinctive appearance and history that is valued by local people and visitors alike.

In Chapeltown, for example, the council is being partnered by English Heritage and the Heritage Lottery Fund, who are providing funds towards repairs in key buildings. These include St Martin, Potternewton (1879–81, Adams and Kelly) (*see* opposite p 1) and its adjacent institute, two of the many religious buildings that give the area such a distinctive character and that bear witness to the role of the area as a home for successive generations of immigrants to the city. In Armley the vast St Bartholomew's (1872, Walker & Athron), with its fine church organ, has been restored with a £1 million grant, while nearby a proposed Townscape Heritage Initiative funded by the Heritage Lottery Fund and the City Council may be able to revive the fortunes of other landmarks such as the former Primitive Methodist Chapel on the corner of Stanningley and Branch Roads (1905, T and C Howdill), now a carpet warehouse, so that they are once again fitting symbols of the pride of the local community.

English Heritage and the Heritage Lottery Fund operate a joint scheme to assist congregations with the repair of their places of worship. In Leeds, funds have been provided to support roof and other repairs at Leeds Parish Church (1831–41, R D Chantrell); Mill Hill Chapel (1847–8, Bowman & Crowther); All Souls, Blackman Lane (1876–80, G G Scott); St Aidan, Roundhay Road (1891–4, Johnson & Crawford-Hick); St Thomas, Stanningley Road (1841, H Rogerson); St James, Seacroft (1845–6, T Hellyer), St Saviour, Ellerby Road (1842–5, J M Derick); City Church, Headingley Lane (1864–6, Cuthbert Brodrick); Holy Trinity, Boar Lane (1721–7, William Etty) and Holy Trinity, Meanwood (1849, William Railton). Development grants have been given recently to St Margaret of Antioch, Cardigan Road (1908–9, Temple Moore) and St Wilfrid, Halton (1937–9, Randall Wells) (*see* pp 30–31), for the preparation of repair schemes.

The great neo-Byzantine shul (prayer hall) of the New Synagogue, Chapeltown Road (1929–32, J Stanley Wright), one of the most spectacular inter-war synagogues in England, has been transformed into the Riley Hall, a performance space for the Northern School of Contemporary Dance. [DP006493]

Realistically, however, public funds cannot secure the future of every historic place of worship. The 'Inspired!' campaign launched in May 2006 by English Heritage with the support of all the major Christian denominations encourages more strategic approaches to be taken on use and maintenance, requiring only modest new funding from government. Where churches have lost their congregations and with them their religious purpose, it ought to be more possible in urban areas to find new uses. Former churches on Woodhouse Lane have been converted to create offices, teaching space, a night club and a bar. The former Leeds New Synagogue on Chapeltown Road provides a home for the Northern School of Contemporary Dance (*previous page*). In these new uses the buildings continue to contribute to the life and appearance of the city and are kept in good repair.

In some cases there is no obvious viable use, and prolonged vacancy can lead to decay and even demolition. The Roman Catholic Oblates order closed Mount St Mary nearly 20 years ago, after housing clearance had greatly reduced the local population. It has stood empty, along with its adjacent presbytery, ever since. In spite of repeated attempts no viable reuse that retains these once fine historic buildings intact has been found. In these circumstances radical options merit consideration, to salvage something from the site's rich past to pass on to the future. An inventive and architecturally exciting housing scheme has recently been proposed, which would at least preserve the chancel and transepts by E W Pugin but replace the decayed nave with new housing.

The spires and minarets of the city's places of worship give a spiritual character to its skyline, reflecting the changing make-up of its population and the movement of faith communities around the city. The towers of Mammon that are beginning to mark the current phase of the city's growth promise a skyline of a different character. We should value our historic places of worship, which tell the stories of our past and present religious observance and which make such a visually rich contribution to the local distinctiveness that gives each place its own identity. We can best demonstrate our care for them by using them well, recognising that adaptation and reuse is part of the history of places of worship in Leeds.

References

Department of the Environment and Department for National Heritage 1994 *Planning and the Historic Environment* (Planning Policy Guidance 15, PPG 15). www.communities.gov.uk

Hammond, P 1960 *Liturgy and Architecture.* London: Barrie & Rockliff

Hastings, A 1994 'The role of Leeds within English religious history' *in* Mason, A (ed) *Religion in Leeds.* Stroud: Alan Sutton, 7.

Office of the Deputy Prime Minister 2005 *Delivering Sustainable Development* (Planning Policy Statement 1, PPS 1). www.communities.gov.uk

Powell, K 1980 *The Fall of Zion: Northern Chapel Architecture and its Future.* London: SAVE Britain's Heritage

Powell, K 1981 *The New Iconoclasts.* London: SAVE Britain's Heritage

Powell, K and De La Hey, C 1987 *Churches: A Question of Conversion.* London: SAVE Britain's Heritage

Wrathmell, S with Minnis, J 2005 Leeds (Pevsner Architectural Guides). New Haven and London: Yale University Press

Further reading

Douglas, J 1996 *Leeds Places of Worship Trail.* Leeds: Leeds Civic Trust

Finnigan, R E and Bradley, G T (eds) 1994 *Catholicism in Leeds: A Community of Faith* 1794–1994. Leeds: Leeds Diocesan Archives

Freedman, M 1995 *Leeds Jewry: A History of its Synagogues.* Leeds 1995

Linstrum, D 1978 *West Yorkshire: Architects and Architecture.* London: Lund Humphries

Mason, A (ed) 1994 *Religion in Leeds.* Stroud: Alan Sutton

Powell, K, Chappell, D and Bosomworth, D 1976 *Leeds Churches 1890–1940.* Leeds: Victorian Society, West Yorkshire Group

Other titles in the Informed Conservation series

Behind the Veneer: The South Shoreditch furniture trade and its buildings. Joanna Smith and Ray Rogers, 2006. Product code 51204, ISBN 9781873592960

The Birmingham Jewellery Quarter: An introduction and guide. John Cattell and Bob Hawkins, 2000. Product code 50205, ISBN 9781850747772

Bridport and West Bay: The buildings of the flax and hemp industry. Mike Williams, 2006. Product code 51167, ISBN 9781873592861

Built to Last? The buildings of the Northamptonshire boot and shoe industry. Kathryn A Morrison with Ann Bond, 2004. Product code 50921, ISBN 9781873592793

Gateshead: Architecture in a changing English urban landscape. Simon Taylor and David Lovie, 2004. Product code 52000, ISBN 9781873592762

Manchester's Northern Quarter. Simon Taylor and Julian Holder, 2007. Product code 50946, ISBN 9781873592847

Manchester: The warehouse legacy – An introduction and guide. Simon Taylor, Malcolm Cooper and P S Barnwell, 2002. Product code 50668, ISBN 9781873592670

Margate's Seaside Heritage. Nigel Barker, Allan Brodie, Nick Dermott, Lucy Jessop and Gary Winter. Product code 51335, ISBN 9781905624669

Newcastle's Grainger Town: An urban renaissance Fiona Cullen and David Lovie, 2003. Product code 50811, ISBN 9781873592779

'One Great Workshop': The buildings of the Sheffield metal trades. Nicola Wray, Bob Hawkins and Colum Giles, 2001. Product code 50214, ISBN 9781873592663

Storehouses of Empire: Liverpool's historic warehouses. Colum Giles and Bob Hawkins, 2004. Product code 50920, ISBN 9781873592809

Stourport-on-Severn: Premier town of the canal age. Colum Giles, Keith Falconer, Barry Jones and Michael Taylor. Product code 51290, ISBN 9781905624362

£7.99 each (plus postage and packing)

To order
Tel: EH Sales 01761 452966
Email: ehsales@gillards.com

Online bookshop: www.english-heritage.org.uk

Inside back cover *The powerful tubular steel cross backed by abstract glass in the fine east window of St Paul, Ireland Wood. [DP027050]*

Back cover *The former Newton Park Union Chapel (1887, Archibald Neil), has been converted to function rooms and a hall for the Sikh community. [IMG 2178]*